Short Walks
The Levels & South Somerset

Robert Hesketh

Bossiney Books

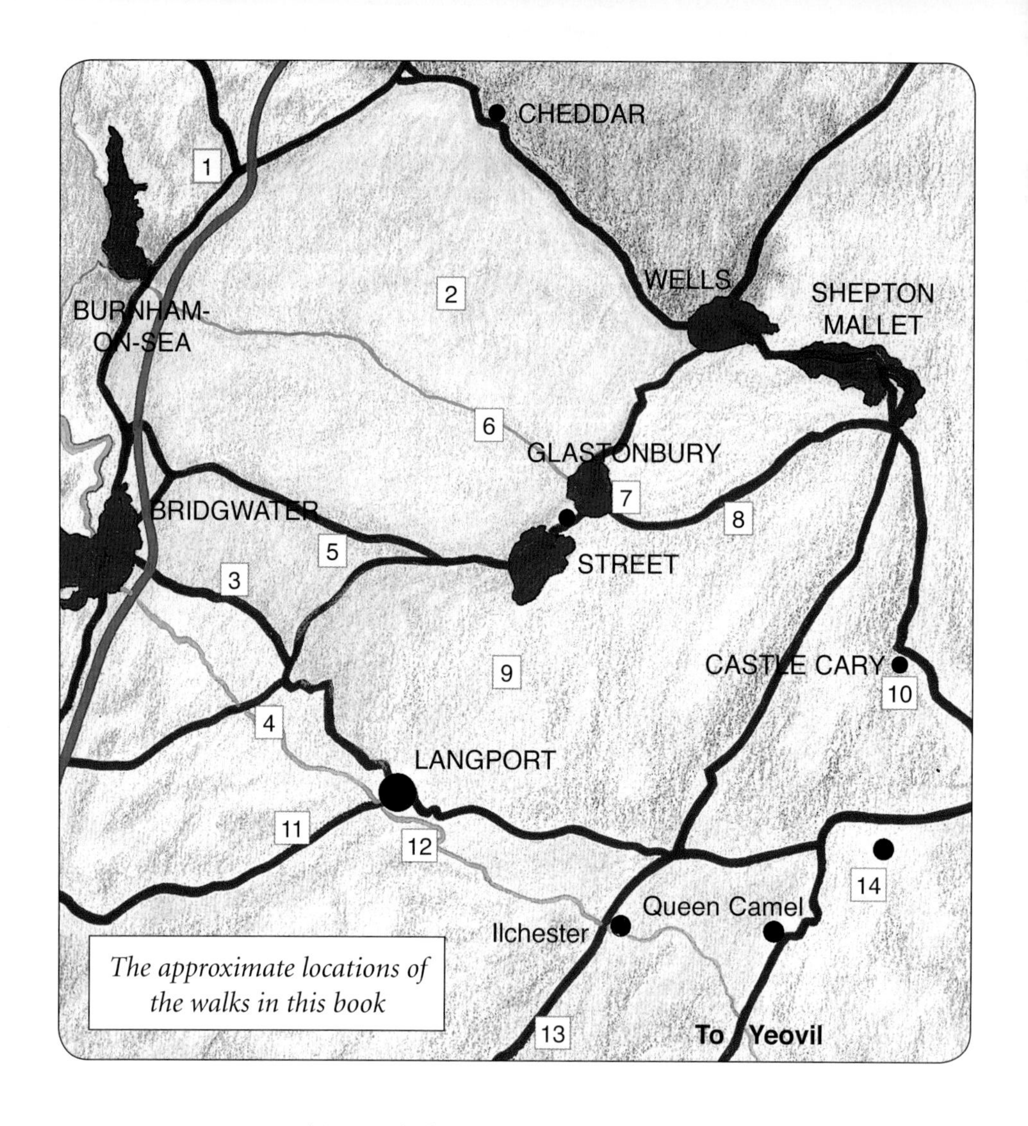

This second edition 2015. First published 2007 by
Bossiney Books Ltd, 33 Queens Drive, Ilkley, LS29 9QW
www.bossineybooks.com

ISBN 978-1-906474-50-8

Acknowledgements

The maps are by Graham Hallowell. Cover based on a design by Heards Design Partnership. The boots on the front cover were kindly supplied by The Brasher Boot Company. The photographs are by the author.

Printed in Great Britain by Latimer Trend & Company Ltd, Plymouth

Introduction

At 5-9km (3-6 miles) the routes in this book can all be walked in a morning or an afternoon. The time you need depends on how fast you walk and how interested you are in what you see – and each walk has several extras, ranging from historic churches and inns to eccentric monuments, from a medieval abbey to an Elizabethan mansion.

Despite the variety and interest of this beautiful area, South Somerset and the Levels are undiscovered country for most walkers. You are quite likely to have many of these routes to yourself. The only drawbacks are that not all gates and stiles are well maintained and some paths become a bit overgrown in summer. I recommend a walking stick.

South Somerset is delightful throughout the year, but winter is a special season on the Levels. Large numbers of waders and wildfowl shelter here and walks such as Westonzoyland (page 8) and Burrow Mump (page 10) offer great birdwatching opportunities.

The corollary is mud – and even flooding after heavy rain. It is always wise to check the local weather forecast and news.

The sketch maps in this book are just that – sketches. You should go equipped with the relevant Ordnance Survey Explorer map (number given with each walk). Numbers 128, 129, 140, 141, 142 and 153 cover various parts of the area and give information on access too.

Walking South Somerset and the Levels is safe and trouble free as long as you are prepared with good walking boots and suitable clothing. Drinking water, map and compass, plus waterproofs and an extra layer are equally essential, together with a comfortable rucksack. Many, including me, add a walking stick, mobile phone and food to the list. Please lock your car and don't leave valuables in it.

Ticks are a potential nuisance, especially in hot, humid weather. Wearing long trousers and socks offers some protection against briars, nettles and these tiny parasites, which can carry a viral infection, Lyme disease. If one attaches itself to you, remove it promptly and carefully with tweezers (being careful not to leave any of it in your skin) to minimize the risk of infection.

Please keep to the paths over enclosed farmland, use (and close) gates as appropriate and keep dogs under control, especially near sheep.

I am sure you will enjoy these walks as I have.

Robert Hesketh

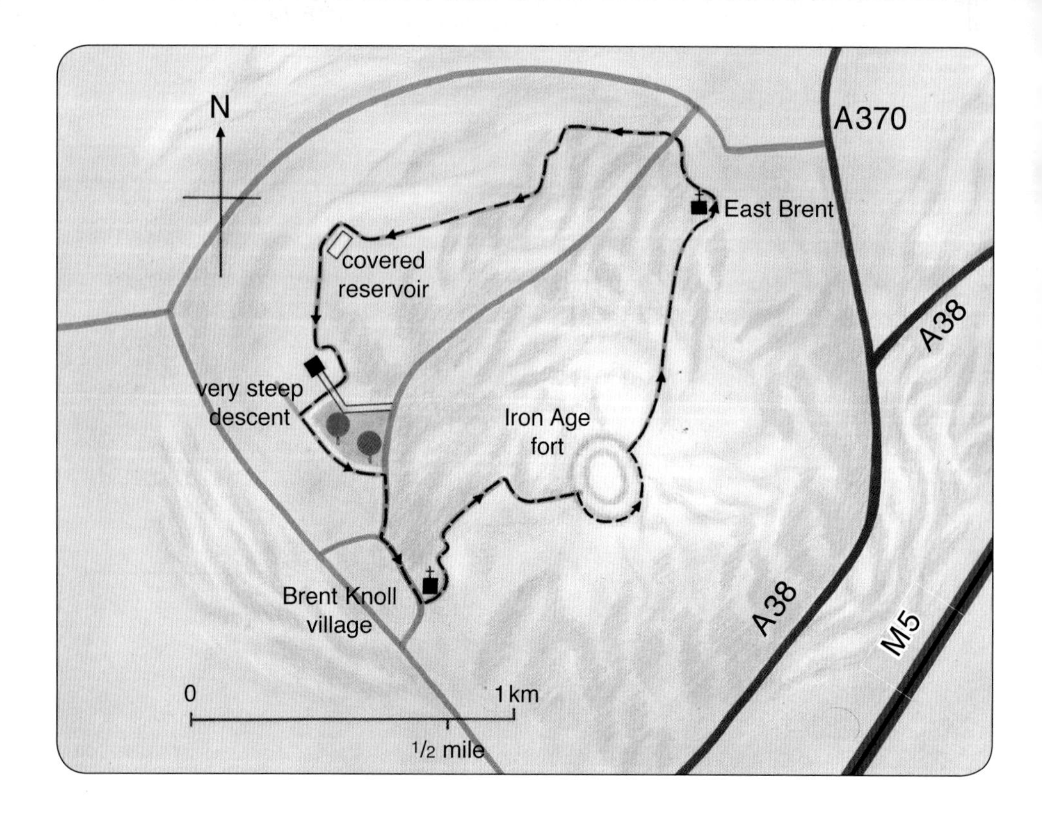

Walk 1 Brent Knoll

Distance: 5km (3 1/4 miles) Time: 1 3/4 hours Map 153
Character: Brent Knoll is an Iron Age fort with high ramparts, and at 139m above sea level commands immense views in all directions. (Take binoculars.) The two historic churches en route are noted for their carved bench ends and ceilings. This moderately demanding walk has one steep ascent, two steep descents and numerous stiles.

Park carefully on the roadside near Brent Knoll church (ST335507). Take the PUBLIC FOOTPATH leading uphill from the east end of the churchyard and follow it round the churchyard. Faced with a stile, don't cross but bear right for THE KNOLL. Keep straight ahead at the kissing gate and follow the fenced path through a gate then up steps to the top of the Knoll. It is said the Devil threw down a shovelful of earth here when digging Cheddar Gorge: certainly it is devilish steep!

Bear right along the rampart past the inscribed stone, then along to the viewing table. Follow the rampart round to a wooden post.

Turn right and follow the well worn path downhill through gates

and a stile towards East Brent's handsome church spire. Follow the path round the school playground to enter the churchyard.

Leave the churchyard by the kissing gate at the far (west) end. Follow the gravelled path through the cemetery to a lane. Cross the lane and enter a PUBLIC FOOTPATH via a stile. Walk straight ahead through a series of small fields, crossing four stiles.

Immediately after a small footbridge, turn left as signed and go through a metal field gate. Cut diagonally right and steeply uphill through the field to meet its upper hedge. (The footpath sign at the metal gate is slightly misleading as to direction.) Continue ahead with the hedge on your right. Leave the field by a stile in the upper hedge near the top. Walk ahead on a clear path, following a nearly straight course over a series of fields, stiles and gates to a covered reservoir.

Cross a stile hidden in the hedge to the right of the reservoir, and follow the enclosed footpath round the perimeter. Then continue ahead with the hedge on your right over another series of stiles and gates to a drive. Cross straight over the drive via a pair of stiles and head very steeply downhill to a stile.

Cross the stile, then continue ahead through a gate and woodland to a lane. Turn right, then left at the road junction to return to Brent Knoll church.

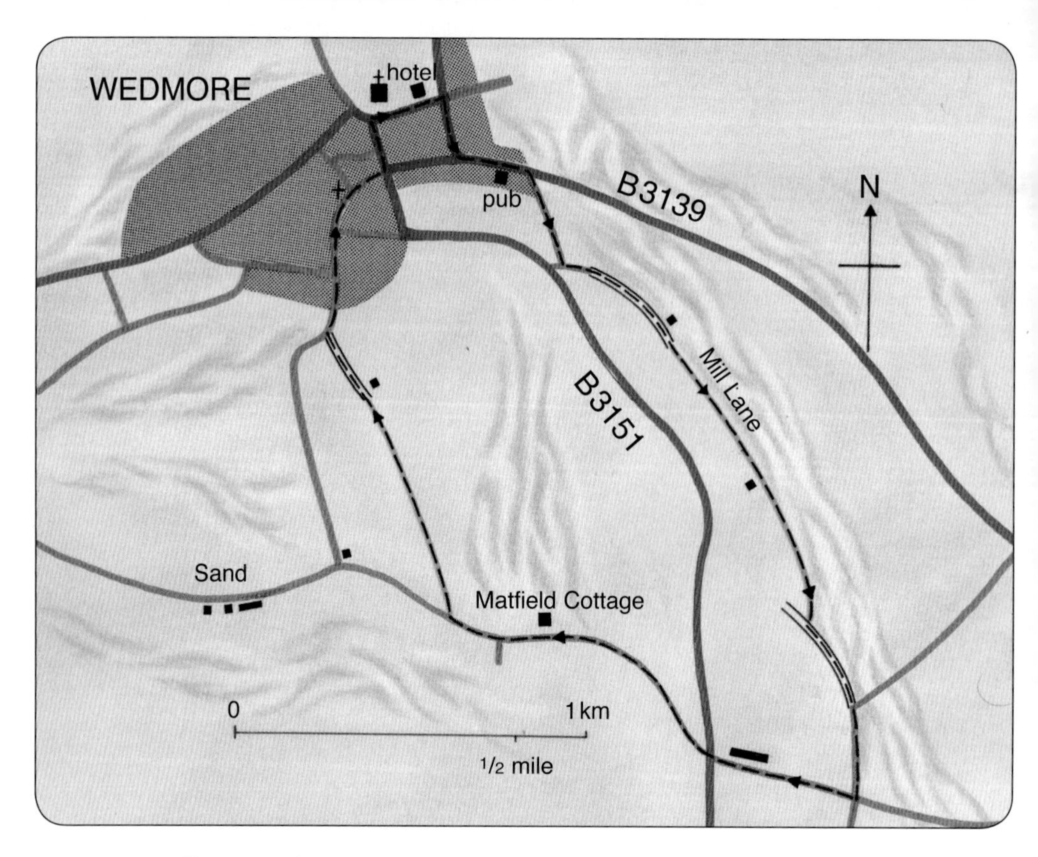

Walk 2 Wedmore

Distance: 5.3km (3¼ miles) Time: 1½ hours Map 141
Character: Wedmore has a fine, large church and many attractive stone buildings. We make a short climb to Mill Lane and there are excellent views over the northern Levels to the Mendips. The return is by quiet lanes and easy footpaths.

Park carefully in Church Street (ST435479). Keep the church (noted for its 1520 wall painting of St Christopher) on your left and walk down the street. Turn right at the junction. At the T-junction, turn left, WELLS. Just past the New Inn, turn right into Mutton Lane. At the top of Mutton Lane, turn left at the No Through Road sign.

Mill Lane is tarred for a short distance only, and later becomes a narrow path. About 1.5km ahead, it joins another track. Continue ahead and maintain the same direction when the track joins a lane. Turn right at the crossroads.

Cross the main road with care, and walk towards SAND for 1km.

Pass a cottage with a red tiled roof. Follow the lane for a further 350 m. Just before a large new cowshed, turn right. Bear left 50 m ahead PUBLIC FOOTPATH. Keep the hedge on your left. Ignore the footpath left. Go through the gate at the far end. Continue on the same course with the hedge on your right. Cross a stile and go through a gate. Continue to a lane.

Turn right onto the lane, and continue ahead at the junction (SHAPWICK GLASTONBURY). Follow the lane right at a chapel and take the second left, GLANVILLE ROAD. Walk ahead to the church.

In AD 878 Wedmore was the scene of a notable adult baptism. Guthrum, the heathen Danish king, accepted the faith and peace with King Alfred, who had defeated him at 'Ethandune' – probably somewhere near Chippenham. According to the Anglo-Saxon Chronicle:

> He [Alfred] fought against the whole host and put them to flight and chased them even unto their stronghold… The chrism-loosing was at Wedmore. And twelve nights abode Guthrum with the king, and many a worthy gift gave he to him and his.

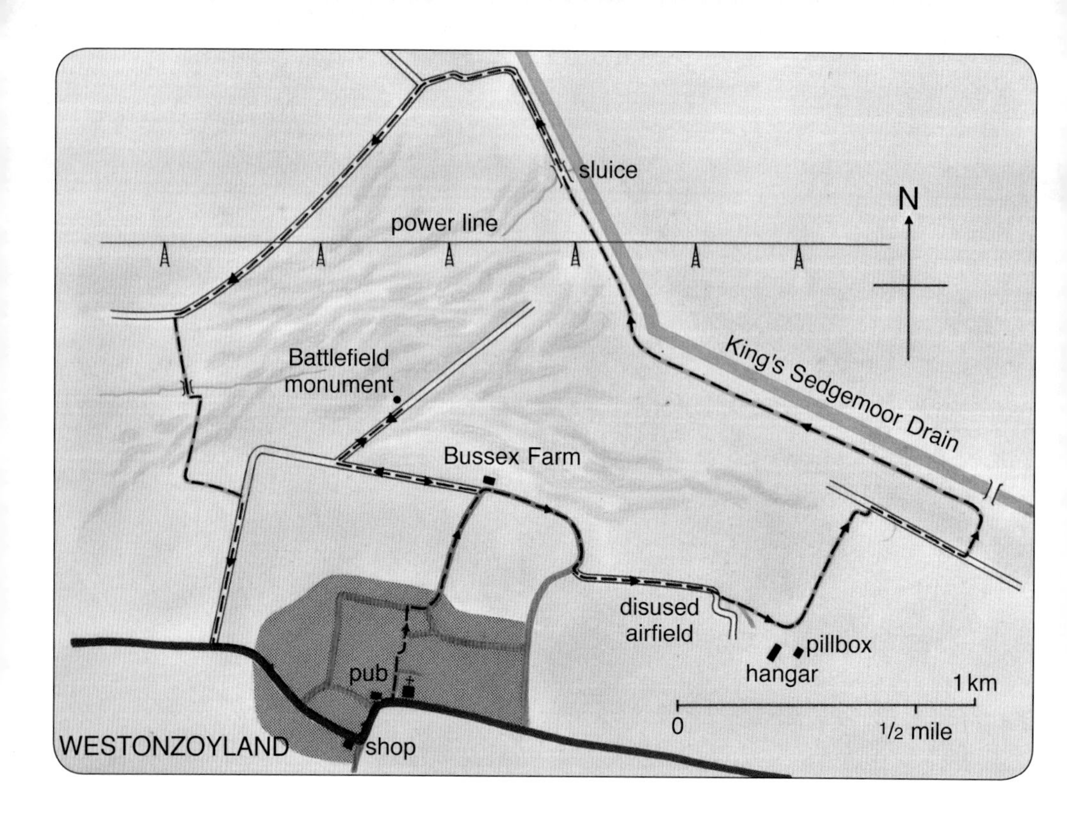

Walk 3 Westonzoyland and the Battle of Sedgemoor

Distance: 9.6 km (6 miles) Time: 3 hours Map 140
Character: This entirely level walk circuits the site of the last battle fought on English soil, Sedgemoor in 1685, now a haven for wetland birds. Take binoculars. The field paths tend to be overgrown in summer. This is the longest walk in the book, and can be extended a further 1.6 km (1 mile) if you wish to visit the battle monument.

Park carefully on the roadside near the church (ST351348). Take CHURCH LANE, to the left of the church. When it turns right, take the footpath ahead between gardens. Arriving at a street, turn right. Follow MONMOUTH ROAD as it curves left following SEDGEMOOR signs.

Battle leaflets are available at Bussex Farm, opposite the helpful display board. To visit the battle monument, turn left onto the drove (a private track but walkers are welcome at their own risk). After 500 m, take the track to the right for 300 m. Then retrace your steps.

Otherwise, follow LINEY ROAD as it bends to the right in front of Bussex Farm. Turn left when the lane bends right 500 m ahead signed

PUBLIC FOOTPATH. Walk ahead on the track through the disused airfield. When the tarmac track turns right, keep left and left again, first on a well-beaten path, then a lesser path parallel to a ditch on your left.

Go through a gate and continue with the ditch on your left. Just before you reach a WW2 pill-box, turn left across a small bridge. Keep the field boundary on your left and and walk ahead through two fields to a gate. Turn right, PUBLIC FOOTPATH. Follow the drove ahead through a gate. Turn left at the next footpath sign and walk to the footbridge, but do not cross it. Turn left and follow the south bank of the King's Sedgemoor Drain for the next 2.25 km, over a series of stiles and under a major power line.

The path becomes a track. Follow it when it curves away from the Drain and ignore side turnings. Cross back under the power line and after a further 400m turn left at the second of two metal gates, 20m before the track makes an S-bend right.

Keep the drainage ditch on your left and walk along the field edge. (Please beware of drops at the edge of this and subsequent paths, which may be hidden by vegetation.) Cross a metal footbridge and turn left, then after 30m right. Keep the hedge on your left to the end of the field, then turn left, and keep the hedge on your right. Turn right onto the track. At the main road, turn left and follow it into Westonzoyland. Turn left at the shop, then right at the Sedgemoor Inn.

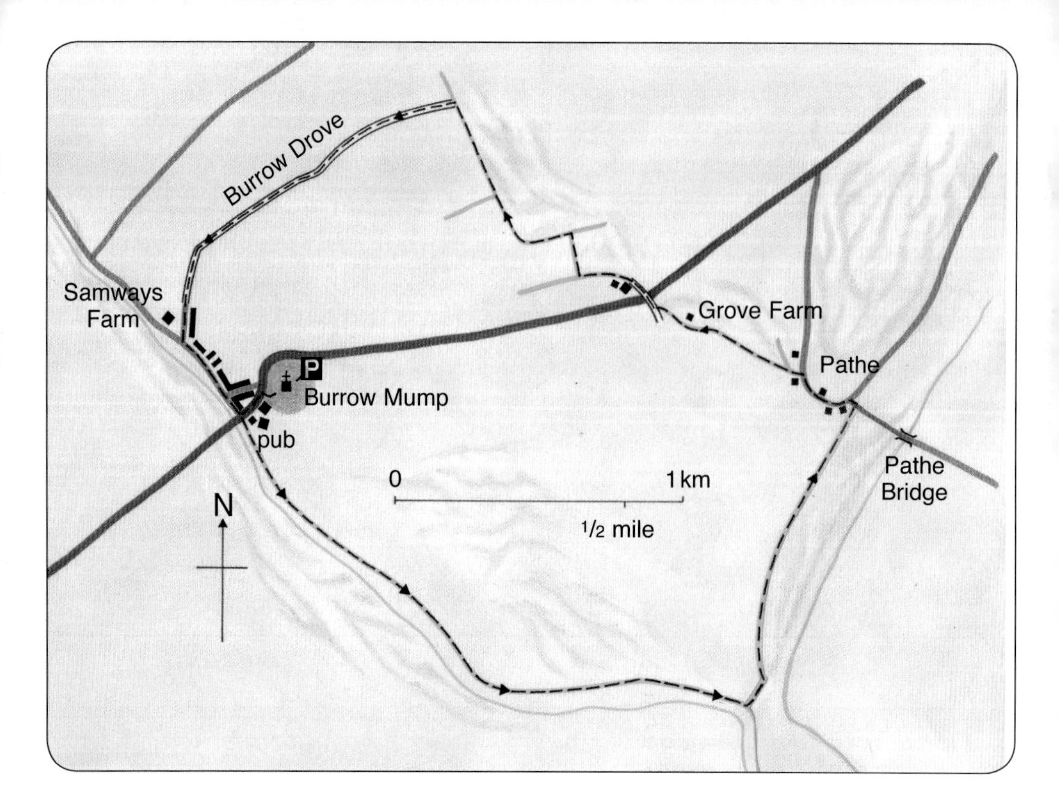

Walk 4 Burrow Mump

Distance: 8km (5 miles) Time: 2¼ hours Map 140
Character: Now crowned with a ruined church, Burrow Mump served as a lookout post for King Alfred when he hid from the invading Danes on the Isle of Athelney, and as a Royalist redoubt during the Civil War. A mere 23m high, the Mump nevertheless dominates Sedgemoor and offers superb views over to the Blackdowns and Mendips. We use riverbank and field paths, rich in bird life. Take binoculars.

Park at the National Trust car park at Burrow Mump (ST 360306). Lock your car and leave no valuables. Climb the Mump – our only ascent. Descend to the far right hand corner of the enclosure. Go through the gate and down the steps to the main road. Turn left.

Immediately after the King Alfred Inn, turn left and follow the track. Signed STATHE PERMISSIVE FOOTPATH 100m ahead, this delightful path follows a raised track along the east bank of the River Parrett. Please stick to the path and keep dogs under control.

Continue for 2.2km (1⅓ miles) via a series of Bristol gates to the far end of the permissive path where the river bends sharply right.

Turn sharp left to cross under the electricity cables. The right of way runs slightly to the left of the river through a series of gates. Arriving at a ditch, keep it and the house on your left to join the lane. Turn left over the bridge and immediately left at the road junction, into Pathe.

Follow the lane as it curves through the hamlet. Just beyond a right hand bend and a converted barn, turn left through a gravelled parking area to a gate. In the field beyond, do not follow the obvious grassy track uphill. Instead drop down the rough bank to a half hidden gate beyond the orchard (not the gate into the orchard). Follow the right edge of the next field to a gate in the corner. Cross the next field, then pass to the left of the barns and Grove Farm. Continue on the path ahead, along the left edge of a rough field to a stile. Turn right and walk to the A361.

Cross with care and walk up the track for 200m to a gate and track junction. Turn right, then after 150m turn left. After a further 220m follow the track as it turns right. Ignore the first turning left, but take the second left. Follow this track for 1.3km to a lane at Samways Farm. Turn left and walk to the King Alfred Inn. Retrace your steps to the car park.

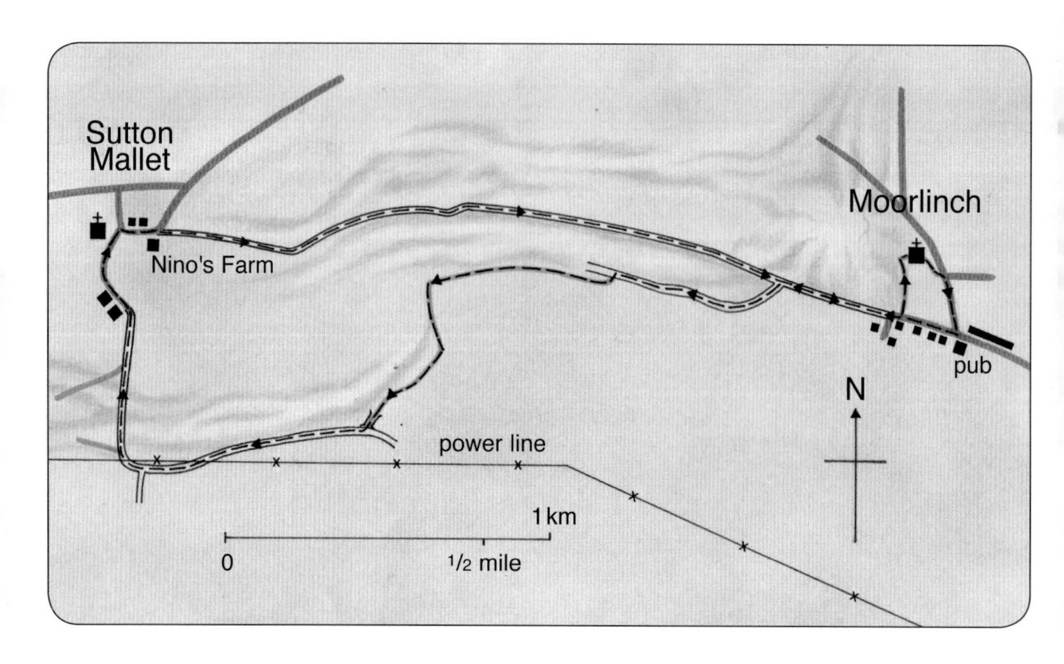

Walk 5 Two Polden villages

Distance: 7.25km (4 1/2 miles) Time: 2 1/4 hours Map 140
Character: From the attractive village of Moorlinch, we take a gentle walk along tracks and field paths to Sutton Mallet and return via a ridge track, offering a broad vista. One of the best views anywhere in the Levels is obtained from Moorlinch churchyard.

Park carefully on the roadside (ST399366) by the Ring of Bells at Moorlinch, a pleasing stone-built inn with exposed beams, wood-burning stoves and period photographs of the village. With the inn on your left, walk ahead down the cul-de-sac lane past an interesting collection of vernacular and modern buildings.

The lane becomes a track. Continue ahead. When the track forks, bear left and walk on for 650m, at which point the track becomes impassably overgrown.

Go through the gap on your left and turn right. Follow the field edge parallel to your previous course, keeping the hedge on your right. At the end of a series of interconnecting small fields go through a kissing gate and turn left along an enclosed path. Go through the gate at the far end.

Turn right and follow the line of cables. Leave the first field by a gap

in the hedge to the left of the next telegraph pole. Cut diagonally left across the next field to exit at the far left corner over a small bridge.

Pause for a view of Moorlinch. Turn right onto the track and continue for 800m. Ignore a left turn, then follow the track sharp right and uphill, ignoring the stile on the left. Stay with the track when it bends left and then right, to Sutton Mallet church.

Turn right. After 90m the lane curves left at Nino's Farm. Leave the lane and walk ahead on a track between hedgebanks for the next 3km to Moorlinch.

Just before reaching the inn, there is a narrow path opposite the imposing stone barn of Townsend Farm. If it is not impossibly overgrown, turn left up it. Climb stone steps and continue uphill and over a stile. Keep the hedge on your right to the church. Built on the highest point in the village, its 13th century tower is a landmark for miles around. Leave by the main church path. Turn right into the lane and return to the start.

For twenty years until 2002, Moorlinch was home to a vineyard but the owners retired and it has now ceased production. There are craft workshops at its former site.

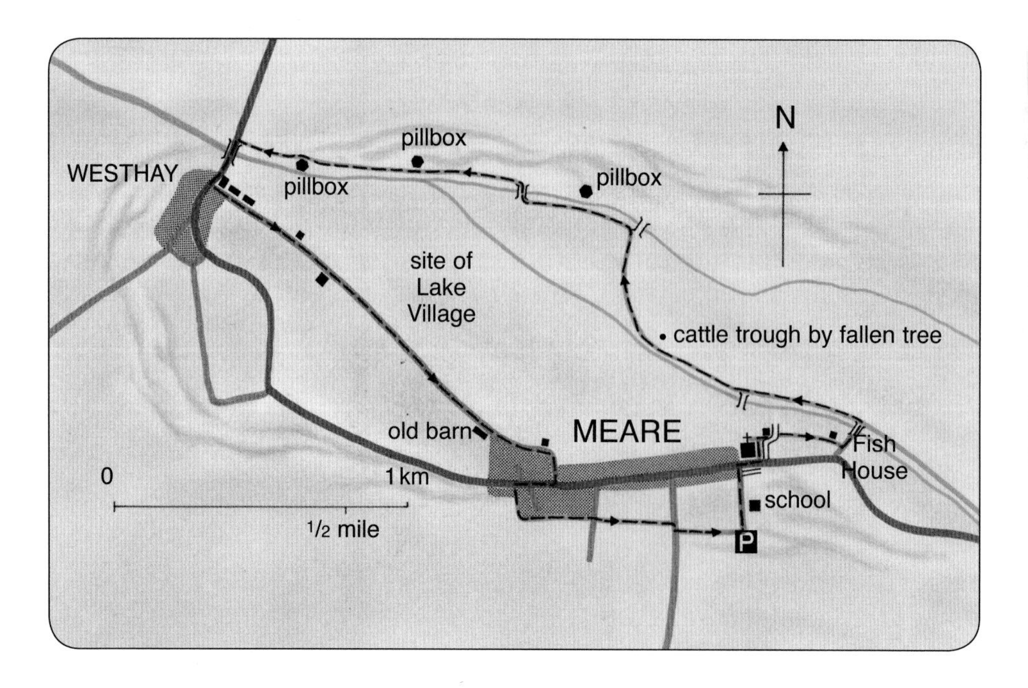

Walk 6 Meare and Westhay

Distance: 6.7 km (4 1/4 miles) Time: 1 3/4 hours Map 141
Character: Much of this classic Levels landscape – rich water meadows, thick with flowers in spring and divided by rhynes and stands of willow – was once underwater as Meare Pool. You will pass St Mary's church, Meare Farm and the Abbot's Fish House, all 14th century.

Park at Muddy Lane car park (ST 455414). Muddy Lane (unsigned) is 50 m west of St Mary's, immediately to the right of a garage, and the car park is at the far end – see map.

Walk back up Muddy Lane to the garage and turn right. Meare's beautiful Perpendicular church has wonderful ironwork on the south door. Take the path between the east end of the churchyard and Meare Farm.

Turn right at the metal gate and walk in front of Meare Farm (where a key is available for the Fish House) and through another gate. Cross the meadow to the Abbot's Fish House. The only surviving monastic fishery building in England, it was probably the house of the chief water bailiff. The hall (living quarters) was on the first floor, overlooking Meare Pool, which had a circumference of 8 km and was not drained until the late 18th century.

Go through the kissing gate and turn left. Cross the bridge and turn left again. Follow the north bank of the River Brue past an arched stone bridge and on to a metal gate. Go through this gate and continue along the bank to a drinking trough, near, at the time of writing, to a fallen tree. Bear 45° right across the field to a gate.

Go through this gate and walk to a footbridge. Don't cross, but turn left and follow the south bank of White's River (noting the World War Two pillbox on the opposite bank) to the next bridge. Cross and turn left along the north bank, past another two pillboxes, to the road.

Turn left across the bridge and pass the Bird in Hand, then turn immediately left into MEAREWAY. Follow this quiet lane past an interesting mix of old cottages. In a field on the left, undistinguished low mounds mark the site of the Iron Age Meare Lake Village. Continue into Oxenpill, and follow the lane when it turns sharp right.

At the T-junction, turn right, walk past DOWN'S ORCHARD and 50m ahead turn left into a PUBLIC FOOTPATH. This runs between gardens, then curves left. Keep the gardens on your left. Continue over a series of small fields, yards and stiles. Cross two lanes and continue in the same direction to the car park.

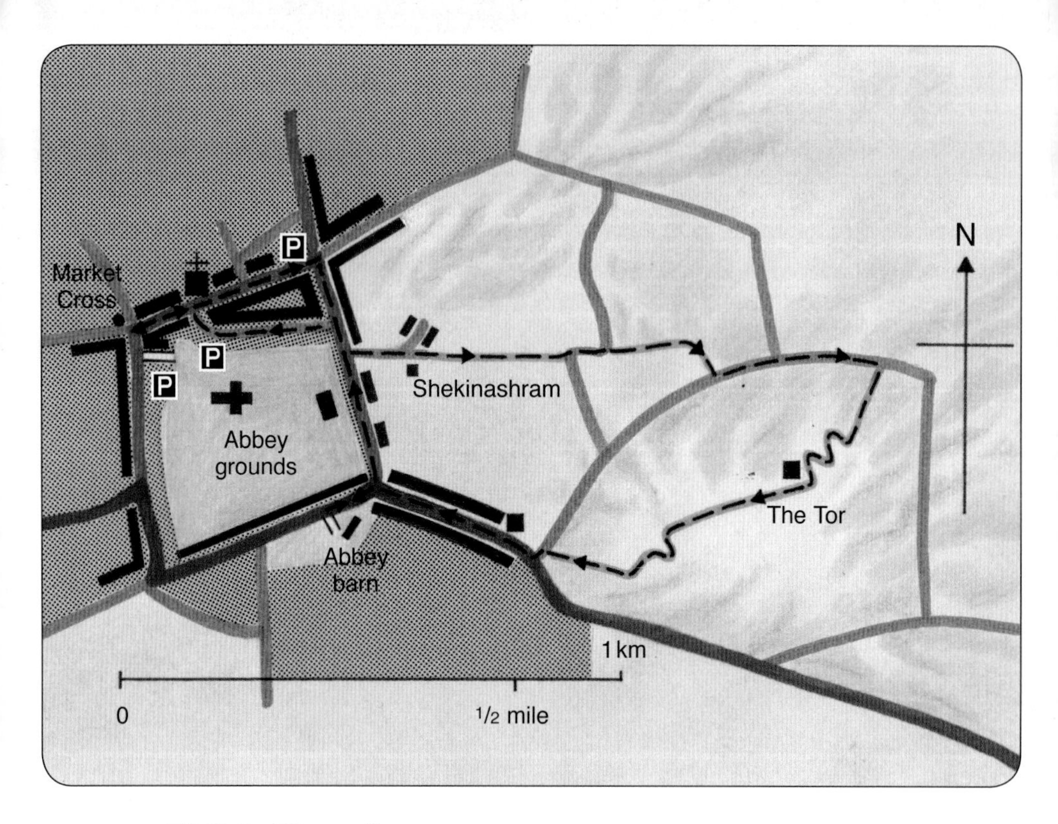

Walk 7 Glastonbury

Distance: 4km (2½ miles) Time: 1¼ hours Map 141
Character: Glastonbury Tor with its 15th century church tower is the most prominent and evocative landmark on the Levels. The stiff climb to the top (158m) is rewarded with magnificent views – take binoculars, and expect it to be cool in the breeze.

The ruined Abbey is one of England's finest and you will pass many other interesting medieval buildings. This is a very popular walk so you are unlikely to be alone!

Glastonbury has several car parks close to the Abbey. With your back to the Abbey entrance, turn right and right again into High Street, passing the George and Pilgrims, the Tribunal (once the Abbey's court-house), and St John's church. All are medieval and worth visiting.

Turn right at the top end of High Street. Take the second turning left, DOD LANE, signed PUBLIC FOOTPATH TO THE TOR. Fork right at the next footpath sign, past the Shekinashram with its Tibetan prayer wheels, and join the footpath.

Continue to a tarmac lane. Walk ahead as signed. Leave the lane when it bends sharply left. Go through the kissing gate ahead onto the footpath and follow it through two further kissing gates. Turn left up the lane to the display board and concreted path leading up to the tor. (Please stay on the path to minimise erosion.)

Use the viewing table to enjoy the panorama – you've earned it. Particularly prominent are Wells and its cathedral, West Pennard church and hill (Walk 8) and the rugged outlines of Mendip, Quantock and Exmoor.

Take the concreted path down to a lane. Turn left and immediately right into CHILKWELL STREET. Walk past the Chalice Well and gardens and along the raised pavement. There are several attractive stone-built cottages; one claims to be 16th century.

At the next junction make a brief foray left for 100m, to see the Abbey barn, dating from about 1500, now part of the Somerset Rural Life Museum. Then retrace your steps and turn left along CHILKWELL STREET. Take the first left into SILVER STREET. Follow this down and round to HIGH STREET. Turn left and retrace your steps to the start.

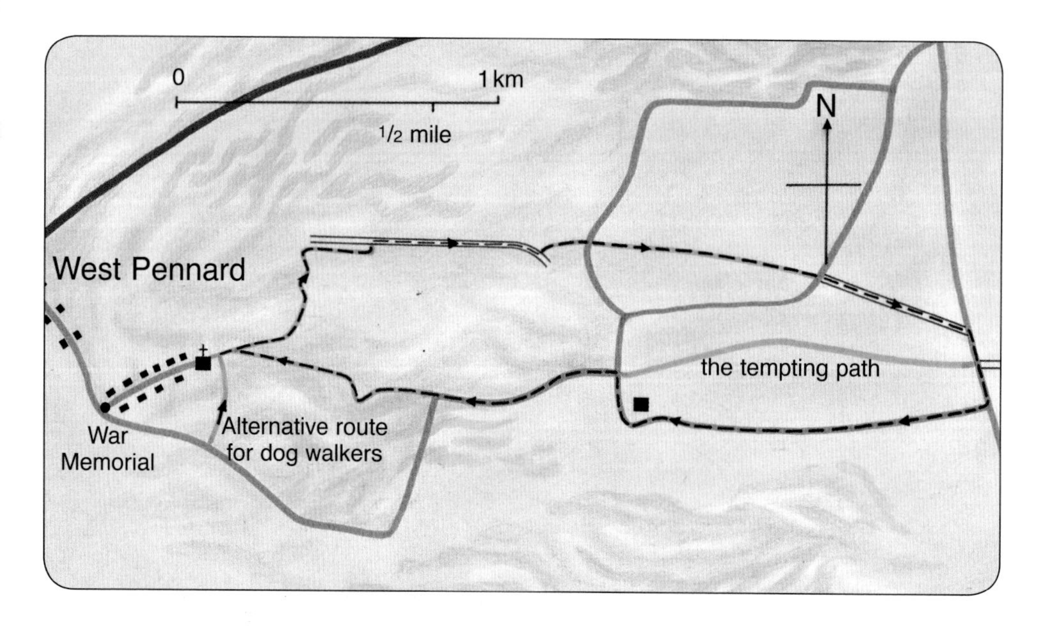

Walk 8 West Pennard

Distance: 5.5km (3 1/2 miles) Time: 1 3/4 hours Map 141
Character: Pennard Hill offers terrific views of Glastonbury Tor, the Mendips and the Levels. The price is a modest climb from West Pennard church, followed by a gentle stroll along field paths and lanes.

Park with care on the lane between the war memorial and St Nicholas's (ST551382), noted for its Perpendicular tower and pepper-pot spire, 16th century rood screen and wonderful ceilings. Walk through the churchyard (see sketch map for an alternative route if you have a dog with you) to a black iron gate.

Take the footpath straight ahead. After 100m the path forks. Take the path straight ahead (not past the water trough) and keep the hedge on your right to a metal gate. Now keep the hedge on your left and walk round the edge of the field to a track.

Turn right and follow the track. When it enters an open field and veers to the right, stay on your original course walking parallel to the hedge on your left. Leave the field by a stile, cross the lane and continue ahead (east) to another stile. The path forks. Keep straight ahead, along a row of isolated trees, to an iron gate. Cross the lane and enter another track, leading to a third lane. Turn right and walk along it.

As the sketch map shows, there is a tempting footpath, starting from a stile opposite the entrance to Pennard Hill Farm, but we have found

it impassable in summer. So unless you're intrepid, follow the lane to a junction and turn right.

Follow this lane for just over 1.2km and turn left at a junction. After 600m, when the lane bends sharp left, walk ahead through a metal gate. Follow the footpath ahead, keeping the hedge on your right, through a large field bisected by a track, to a metal gate.

Turn right and keep the hedge on your left for just 40m, then turn left through a gate. Cut diagonally across the field to a stile and a lovely view of West Pennard. Head back to the church keeping the field edge on your right.

Walk 9 Dundon

Distance: 7.5km (4½ miles) Time: 2½ hours Map 141
Character: The high point of this gentle walk is the modest ascent of Lollover Hill (90m) rewarded by panoramic views. Dundon is a pretty stone and thatch village. The walk can be shortened by 600m if you omit the visit to the Castlebrook Inn.

Park by Dundon church (ST479325), noted for its original painted wagon roof, Jacobean pulpit and the 1700-year-old yew in the churchyard. Walk down the lane and turn right on the footpath for LOLLOVER HILL. Turn right at the track ahead, and follow it uphill to a gate.

Divert left from the track, now a footpath, to the trig. point on Lollover Hill. Return to the path. Go through a gate and walk ahead with the hedge on your right. Go through a gate and continue ahead, following the lower edge of the field as it curves left. At the far corner, go through a metal gate and walk ahead with the hedge on your left.

Turn left through a gate at the end of the field. Cross another field and stile. Continue up an enclosed track for 1 km. Turn right along the lane, past Middle Farm.

Just beyond Cook's Farm, turn right at a stile (marked with a yellow arrow) and leave the field by a stile in the far left corner. Walk ahead with the hedge on your left to another stile. Continue through the yard of Decoy Farm and along the track ahead. When the track turns left, cross a stile and continue diagonally across a field, a stile and a second field to a pair of stiles. Cross these and turn left, keeping the hedge on your left. Climb two more stiles and continue through an orchard, then along the track ahead to a lane.

Cross over (slightly to the left) and continue ahead (PUBLIC FOOTPATH HAM LANE) through a metal gate. Keep the hedge on your right through a series of small fields separated by stiles. On your left is Dundon Hill fort: there is no access.

Where the path meets a hedge at right angles, you have a choice. 1. To visit the Castlebrook Inn (temporarily closed for refurbishment) turn right through a metal gate, walk ahead to the road and turn left (carefully!) to the inn. Then retrace your steps to the path junction. 2. If you intend to omit the inn, turn left and keep the hedge on your right. Don't take the footpath on your right but walk ahead on the same course. The last part of the path is paved and leads past the school. Turn left onto the lane, then right back to the start.

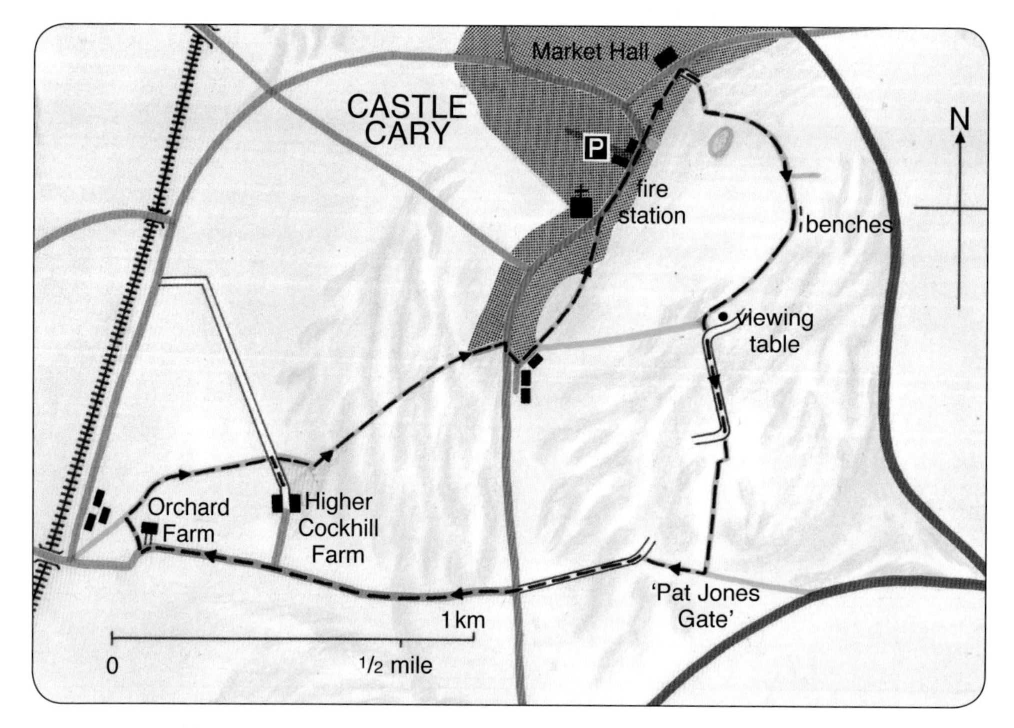

Walk 10 Castle Cary

Distance: 5.5 km (3 1/2 miles) Time: 1 3/4 hours Map 142
Character: Castle Cary, with its Ham stone buildings, horse pond, market hall and lock-up, is a pleasing little town. The climb to Lodge Hill is rewarded with great views over the town and the Levels to Glastonbury Tor and the Mendips.

Turn left out of the signed car park by the fire station, then left again. Cross the road to the horse pond, graced by a bronze statue of a swan. Bear right and carry on as far as the handsome George Hotel.

Opposite the George is the exuberantly Victorian Market Hall, and behind that the 'pepper-pot' lock-up of 1779.

Turn right up PADDOCK DRAIN, an alley by the side of the George, for LODGE HILL. The path climbs to a very narrow kissing gate. Keep left here to pass the rather faint remains of the 24 m square Norman keep. Built by the Perceval family, for centuries a power in Somerset, the castle withstood two sieges in the reign of Stephen (1135-1154) but fell into decay.

Approaching the summit of Lodge Hill, ignore the path straight on and bear right past two thoughtfully provided benches. Continue

past a telescope and viewing table. The path soon divides. Turn left through the gate bearing the Leland Trail waymark. Walk ahead along the track.

When it turns right, continue ahead for 100m, then bear right through a gate (waymarked) and head for an electricity pole.

Just beyond it, the Leland trail turns left at the 'Pat Jones Gate'. We turn right, keeping the fence on our left. Cross a stile and turn left down a farm track. Cross the main road and walk ahead for COCKHILL.

Just past the entrance to Orchard Farm, turn right over a stile. Cross a small field then turn right across a stile to walk behind the farm. Go through a gate, cross a third stile and bear right, keeping the fence on your right. At the next stile blue arrows point both ways. Ignore the arrows. Cross the track and go through the footpath gate ahead. Head for the top left corner of the field. Cross a pair of stiles and walk ahead as signed. Leave the field by the stile in the top left corner.

Turn right at the main road. Take the first left, SOUTH BANK then left again into PARK AVENUE. Go through the iron kissing gate at the end and keep left. Follow the path, and then a street, down to the church which, unusually for Somerset, has a steeple. Parson Woodforde, the diarist, was curate here and recorded everyday life in Castle Cary from 1763 to 1771. Walk ahead along Park Street, back to the car park.

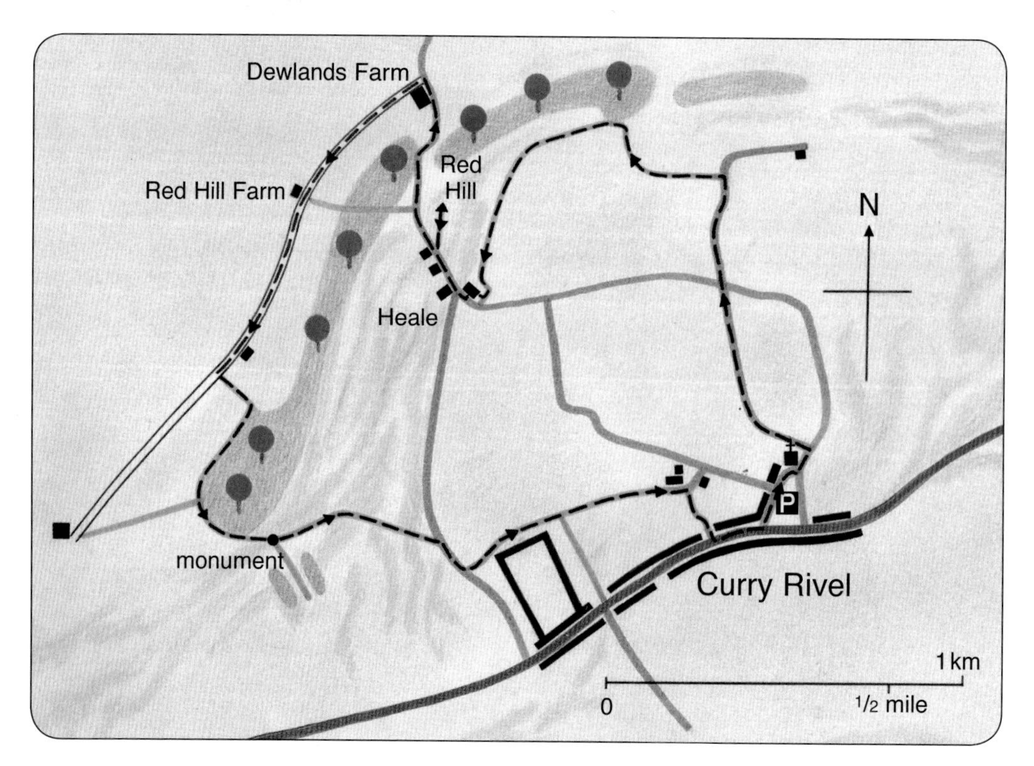

Walk 11 Curry Rivel

Distance: 6.1 km (3¾ miles) Time: 2 hours Map 128
Character: Enjoy superb views of the Levels from both Red Hill and the 42 m high Burton Pynsent monument. (Fortunately you can't climb it!) Curry Rivel has a beautiful church and the Old Forge, a thatched inn with a medieval cellar. One steep ascent. Birdwatching, so take binoculars.

Turn right out of the signed public car park in Curry Rivel (ST 391252) and walk past the Old Forge. Follow the lane to the right of St Andrew's, a classic 15th century Somerset church with Ham stone dressings. Turn left, BUTT LANE. At the crossroads continue ahead for 400 m.

Bear left on a footpath. This leads between hedges, along the edge of a wood and over a stile. Continue with the hedge on your left. Some 250 m before farm buildings turn left through the hedge gate and immediately right along the field edge to a lane. Turn right and walk ahead, ignoring the turning to Curry Rivel. Divert right for 100 m at the National Trust sign for RED HILL to gain a fine view over the Levels.

Return to the lane and follow it downhill to Dewlands Farm. Turn left on a concrete track, NO UNAUTHORISED VEHICLES.

The RSPB bird reserve, best seen in winter, lies to the right. Walk ahead for 1 km to a single-storey brick and tile cottage. About 50 m beyond the cottage, turn left over a stile (well disguised by weeds and trees at the time of writing).

Half way up the field ahead, turn right over a stile. Cross the orchard to another stile. Follow the path along the edge of the wood and over another stile. The next stile is on your right. Do not cross it, but follow the path round to the left and uphill through trees to the Burton Pynsent monument.

Erected by William Pitt in memory of his benefactor Sir William Pynsent (whom he never met), it was designed by 'Capability' Brown in the Roman Doric style and cost £2000 in 1767.

Follow the path through the grass east from the monument (not the path south-east between the stands of trees). This leads through a kissing gate into a well-beaten path and on via another kissing gate to a lane.

Turn right and after 150 m left onto PUBLIC FOOTPATH. Keep the hedge on your left to a kissing gate, then walk ahead with the fence and houses on your right. At the footpath junction continue ahead over a stile towards the church tower. Continue in the same direction via two kissing gates and a stone stile to a stone-and-tile cottage. Where the track bends left, turn right through yet another kissing gate. Turn left onto the main street and left again for the car park.

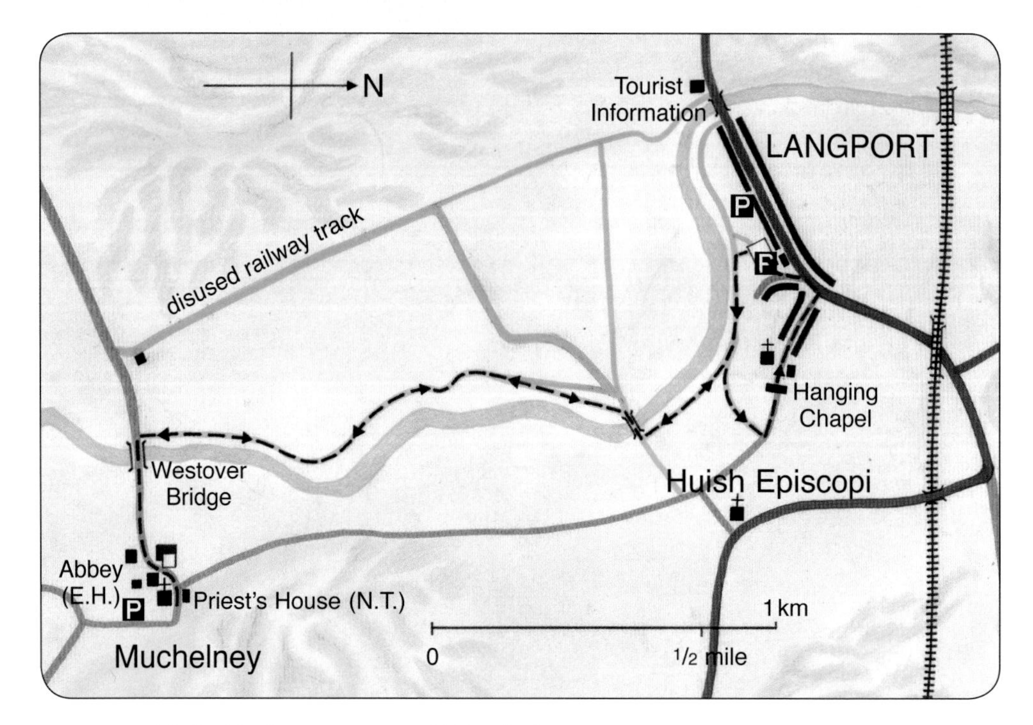

Walk 12 Langport and Muchelney

Distance: 7.6km (4¾ miles) Time: 1¾ hours Map 129

Character: This easy, level there-and-back route follows a riverside path to Muchelney, with its Abbey and medieval Priest's House. The Almonry is a café and the church has a remarkable painted ceiling. On the return journey we divert to see Langport's Hanging Chapel.

Start from the Town Square car park in the centre of Langport. At the time of writing, it offers 2 hours free parking so if you mean to visit the Abbey, you will need to use the long stay car park, further along the main street towards the river. Leave from the far end of the car park and turn left along the bank towards BLACK BRIDGE. Continue with the River Parrett on your right. Turn right across Huish Bridge.

From Huish Bridge take the path left, MUCHELNEY. Continue to Westover Bridge.

Cross Westover Bridge and enter Muchelney. If you want to visit the Abbey (English Heritage, fee) take the signed entrance on the right. Otherwise follow the lane round to the church and the thatched Priest's House opposite, which dates from 1308 (National Trust, rather limited opening hours). The church has a remarkable ceiling with bare bosomed angels.

Retrace your footsteps to Westover Bridge. Take the footpath on the far bank, HUISH BRIDGE, and continue for 1.75km. Turn right over Huish Bridge then start retracing your steps towards Langport. Take the first turning right over a footbridge. The path crosses a field and a ditch then rises between houses to a road.

Turn left and walk to the right of the Hanging Chapel, Langport's guild chapel standing on a bridge. Continue past All Saints and bear right down to the main street. Turn left and return to the car park.

Muchelney is said to have been founded in 939. It was refounded in the 11th century as a Benedictine abbey. The Abbot's Lodging still stands, a complete Tudor house with a magnificent fireplace and a wall painting, whilst the monks' two-storey thatched latrine represents state-of-the-art medieval sanitation.

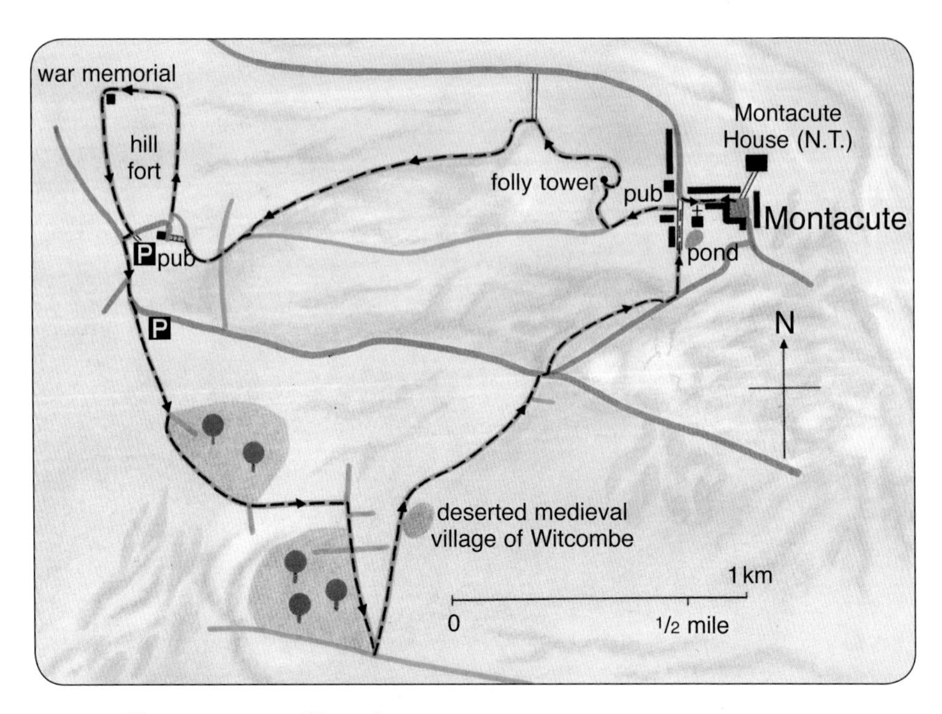

Walk 13 Ham Hill and Montacute

Distance: 7.5 km (4 1/2 miles) Time: 2 1/2 hours Map 129
Character: This route combines great views with a wealth of historic interest, including one of Britain's largest fortified settlements and a village of golden stone. Some ups and downs, but only one steep ascent.

Park at the Ham Hill Country Park (ST 479169) where 5 km of ramparts enclose the remains of 2500 years of successive settlement. From the Prince of Wales pub, go through a small wooden gate and walk north on the rampart path, then round westward past the war memorial and south to meet a tarmac track. Turn right, then left up the lane.

Pass a viewpoint and a side road, then bear right through a car park to join a footpath, LIBERTY TRAIL LYME REGIS. Ignore side turnings. At a T-junction of paths, turn right and downhill, LIBERTY TRAIL. At the bottom of the hill turn left onto the footpath, WITCOMBE LANE. This leads up through the coombe (valley), where the deserted medieval village of Witcombe is marked by hummocks and ridges. From here the path bears right, climbing steadily. Bear left on a track along the top of the field to a stone information stand.

Follow the track ahead to a lane. Take the footpath ahead of you, to the left of HOLLOW LANE. This footpath runs parallel to the lane and

offers a superb view of Montacute. When the path returns to the lane, turn left and almost immediately left again onto PUBLIC BRIDLEWAY MONTACUTE CHURCH. This leads by the old Priory Gatehouse, monastic pond and dovecote to the church and King's Arms. Turn right down MIDDLE STREET to the square and Montacute House (National Trust).

Retrace your steps to the King's Arms and turn left. At the entrance to the Gatehouse, turn right, HEDGECOCK HILL WOOD. The path climbs. After 250m turn right over a stile and follow the steep path to the top of St Michael's Hill, at 139m the *mons acutus* (steep hill) that gave Montacute its name.

A motte and bailey castle once stood here. Now the hill is crowned by a folly tower dated 1760. A spiral stair leads to the top.

Retrace your steps from the folly for 100m and bear left when the path forks. Follow it downhill to a stile. Cut diagonally right (LELAND TRAIL) across the field to a gate and turn left along a track. When the track forks, keep right along the lower edge of Hedgecock Hill. Ignore side turnings. At the top of some steps turn right, then left up steps to return to the Prince of Wales.

The inn is thought to have been a quarry manager's house, dating from about 1830. There is a collection of photographs showing Ham Hill as a working quarry around 1900. The stone was lifted with antique winches and cranes and moved by horse and wagon.

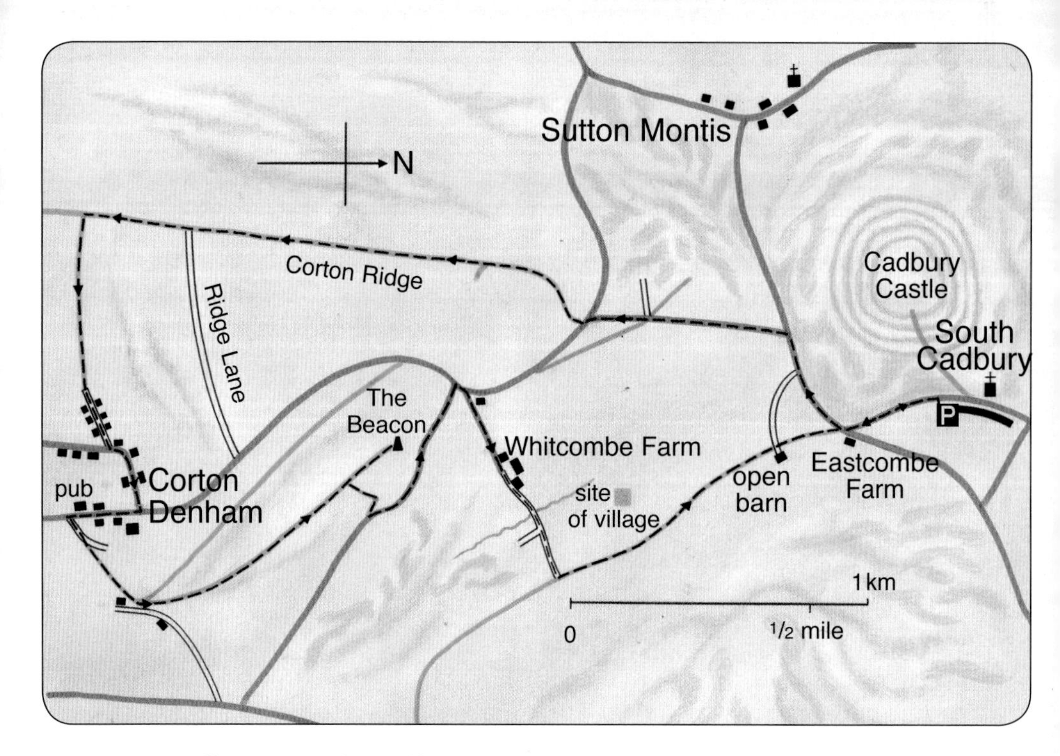

Walk 14 South Cadbury and Corton Denham

Distance: 9km (5¾ miles) Time: 2¾ hours Map 129
Character: This walk offers splendid panoramas of South Somerset, the Mendips and the Levels. Two ascents, neither very demanding.

The walk can be combined with visiting Cadbury Castle, an exceptionally impressive hill fort, re-used in the post-Roman period and strongly identified with King Arthur.

Turn left out of the car park in South Cadbury (ST 632253). Ignore side turnings and continue ahead on CHURCH ROAD until you reach a turning for SHERBORNE. Turn left here.

At a T-junction turn left and immediately right on PUBLIC BRIDLEWAY. The path climbs and great views open out.

Follow the path along the western flank of Parrock Hill then through a wooden gate and south along the Corton Ridge (Macmillan Way waymarks). Continue on the same course when you reach a track to your left, between two metal gates, and after a further 400 m turn left up steps. The path cuts eastward across fields.

Arriving at a lane, turn left and follow it round to a T-junction by the church. Turn right and walk past the Queen's Arms.

Almost immediately, turn left up a tarred lane. After 100m, take the footpath through a gate on the right.

Climb steeply towards the top of the ridge. Just before a metal field gate, the path forks. One path turns left. Take the next path above (see sketch map) which bears left, but don't go through the gate. Now follow the path up to and along the line of the ridge to the Beacon (196m), crowned by a trig. point and a red aircraft warning light. It offers a stunning view over Cadbury Castle's concentric defences.

Retrace your steps for 150m to the corner of a fenced enclosure. Turn left along the fence. Turn right at the fence corner, then sharp left onto a lane. Walk downhill to a junction, and turn right, then right again onto WITCOMB FARM LANE.

Continue past a preserved waterwheel, through the yard and along a track. Turn right, cross a ford and walk uphill to a T-junction. Turn left. A deserted medieval village lies on your left, but its bumps are not readily discerned when crops are growing. Cross four stiles to a lane. Turn right and retrace your steps to the car park.

To visit Cadbury Castle, continue along the lane for 100m and turn left up a footpath.

Tourist Information Centres

Bridgwater 01278 436438
Burnham-on-Sea 01278 787852
Cartgate Picnic Site 01935 829333
Cheddar 01934 744071
Glastonbury 01458 832954
Langport 01458 253527
Sedgemoor Services 01934 750833
Street 01458 447384
Taunton 01823 336344
Yeovil 01935 462781
Weston-super-Mare 01934 417117

Footpath enquiries

General: 0845 3459155 www.somerset.gov.uk/ete/rightsofway/

South Somerset Council: 01935 462462
countryside@southsomerset.gov.uk

Sedgemoor District Council: 0845 408 2540

Some other Bossiney walks books

Shortish walks on Exmoor (5-9km walks)
Shortish walks near Taunton (5-9km walks)
Shortish walks – Quantocks and Mendips (6-8km walks)
Really short walks – Exmoor and Brendon (3-6km walks)
The Somerset Coast – Beaches and walks (3-8km walks)
Shortish walks in east Devon (5-8km walks)
Really short walks – east Devon coast (3-6km walks)

All the walks in this book were checked prior to printing – after the serious floods of 2014 – at which time the instructions were correct. However, changes can occur in the countryside over which neither the author nor publishers have any control. Please let us know if you encounter any serious problems.